Knit to Amaze

A Visual Guide to Knitting Amazing Fingerless Mittens, Knee Warmers, Kitchen Cloths & Coasters

By

Helen Mao

Publishing House

Cover design

Robin Goodnight

First Edition

TABLE OF CONTENTS

INTRODUCTION

Congratulations! Since you are reading this, I can safely assume you already know the basics of knitting and that you have mastered the basic steps of knitting and are ready for your next challenge: simple yet "more-advanced-than beginner" projects that are fun to make and use. You should not feel intimidated once you realize that all knitting projects–from the easiest square piece to the most complicated sweater–are based on the two foundation steps you already know:

- The **knit** stitch
- The **purl** stitch

And of course, you already know how to start a project ...

- **Cast on** stitches

... And finish your masterpiece (again, no matter how small or large, it is your work of art)

- **Cast off** stitches

Every project is a variation on different combinations of the knit and the purl stitches–obviously some combinations more elaborate than others. I have found, nonetheless, that some finished products that look fancy and complicated actually are not; they're just interesting variations on combinations knit stitches and purl stitches. Throw in your choice of various yarn types based on:

- **Colors** (bright, earth tone, pastel, mixed, etc.)
- **Fiber** (acrylic, cotton, wool, combinations of these)
- **Texture** (regular, ribbon, bouclé, chenille, railroad ribbon, faux fur, and more)
- **Weight or size** (fine or sport-weight, light worsted or double-knit/DK, medium worsted, bulky or chunky, jumbo or super chunky)

Also, think about all the different needle sizes that exist to make stitches small and fine or medium or large and loopy … and you will see where variety and creativity in knitting projects are born!

Within all this freedom of choice, of course, you'll need to follow your project pattern's prescription of needle size and yarn type, but otherwise, you can "fancy up" or "dress down" any project.

Do your hands ever feel slightly cold—not enough to pull on full-fledged gloves or thick mittens, but just chilly enough for a little covering? Or could your knees could use a soft, warm hug that keeps in body heat?

If you answered "yes" to either (or both) of these questions, put your new knitting expertise and try these two quick, moderately easy, and ultimately satisfying projects: Fingerless Mittens and Knee Warmers.

All you need for these projects are basic knitting supplies, just knitting needles, yarn, a stitch counter, stitch markers, and a large-eye blunt needle. In each chapter focused on a specific project, I'll tell you exactly what size and kind (straight vs. circular) needles and yarn type you will need.

General knitting term abbreviations include:

K: knit
K#: knit assigned number of stitches
P: purl
P#: purl assigned number of stitches

Tip: Any time you are not sure of a knitting term, look it up on the internet: knitting websites and YouTube demonstrations can be incredibly helpful educational resources. Also, basic knitting books like *Knitting Basics for Beginners* by Karina Gale make very handy reference sources.

CHAPTER ONE: FINGERLESS MITTENS

Cozy and convenient, fingerless mittens keep your hands warm but leave your fingers free to move and complete tasks without getting in the way. Get things done without sacrificing comfort!

These fingerless mittens are perfect for wearing while typing at the computer, texting on the phone, practicing piano, holding a book and turning pages while reading, taking ballet class, and more.

SUPPLIES YOU WILL NEED

Before you begin working on the Fingerless Mittens, gather the following materials:

- One skein (at most 5 ounces, 251 yards) of medium worsted weight (4) yarn–acrylic, acrylic-wool blend, or wool. Personally, I like acrylic because it is soft and warm.
- One pair of size 8 straight knitting needles
- Two stitch markers: pictured are more than two so you can see different sizes; (optional: you can hang "earring-like" decorations from the circular stitch markers like those pictured)
- One large-eye blunt darning needle
- On row counter (optional and not pictured: use whichever style you like, e.g., circular on-the-needle, hand, pendant, etc.)

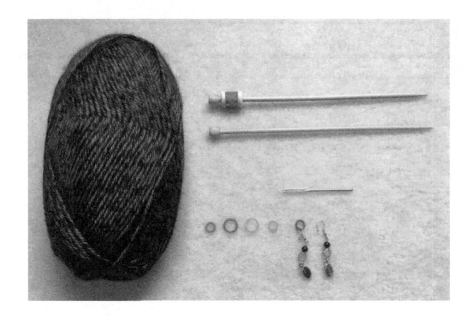

KNITTING TERMS USED IN THIS CHAPTER

Knitting abbreviations and instructions for terms needed in this pattern include:

M1: Make one stitch. Add or increase by one knit stitch by lifting the horizontal thread lying between needles and placing it onto left needle. Knit this new stitch through the back loop, and you have created one new stitch. YouTube has many helpful demonstrations under "M1 knitting".

PM: Place marker on needle

SM: Slip marker from one needle onto the other

This pattern is for one size, but you are free to adjust it (length-wise, width-wise) if you wish. The gauge is 18 stitches by 16 rows equaling about four square inches in stockinette stitch.

Be sure to check your gauge. If you end up needing to knit fewer stitches and rows to make a four-inch square, try using smaller size needles.

If you end up needing to knit more stitches and rows to make a four-inch square, try using a larger size needle.

ACTUAL STEP BY STEP PROCESS

You'll create the project from the bottom edge and work upward.

This pattern can be used for both the left-hand and right-hand fingerless mittens, but if you would like for the side seam to be positioned under each hand) when you wearing the finished mitten, then use those directions for **the upper body hand covering/thumb gusset section of the left mitten.**

Step 1: Cast on 28 stitches.

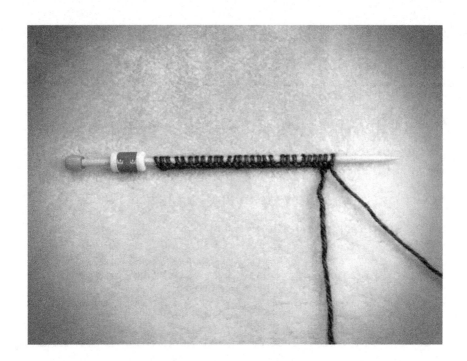

Step 2: To create the bottom ribbing, work K2, P2 (rib stitch), for about 1 inch (6 rows).

Step 3: Then, to create the mitten's lower half (i.e., the section that covers the wrist), work in stockinette stitch for about three inches (another 18 rows).

Step 4: Now you're ready to create the upper body hand covering/thumb gusset.

    a. <u>Row 1</u> (This is on the mitten's right- or out-facing side): K1, PM (place a marker on the needle)

M1 (make one stitch)

K6,

M1,

PM (place second marker on needle)

Then work K to end of row. Since the beginning with 28 cast-on stitches, you have increased or added two new stitches, bringing the total number of stitches in this row to 30.

b. <u>Rows 2-4</u>: Continue in stockinette stitch.

c. <u>Row 5</u>: K1, SM, M1, knit to next marker, M1, SM, knit to end of row. You've increased or added two new stitches to this row, bringing the total number of stitches in this row to 32.

d. <u>Rows 6-8</u>: Continue in stockinette stitch.

e. <u>Row 9</u>: repeat row 5. You've added two new stitches/increase this row to 34 stitches total.

f. <u>Rows 10-12</u>: Continue in stockinette stitch.

g. <u>Row 13</u>: Repeat row 5. You've added two new stitches/increase this row to 36 stitches total, including 14 stitches between markers.

h. <u>Row 14:</u> (WS) Purl to marker, remove marker, P2, bind off 10 stitches for thumb opening, P2, remove marker, and purl to end of row. You should have 26 stitches at the end of this row.

    i.   <u>Row 15</u>: (RS) Knit, casting on 2 stitches over bound off stitches of previous row.

HOW TO CAST ON STITCHES IN THE MIDDLE OF A ROW

This YouTube video:

<u>https://www.youtube.com/watch?reload=9&v =bTgT7kE1c_k&feature=youtu.be</u>

This video is very helpful in explaining and demonstrating the technique described and pictured below.

Turn over the work so the purl side is facing up.

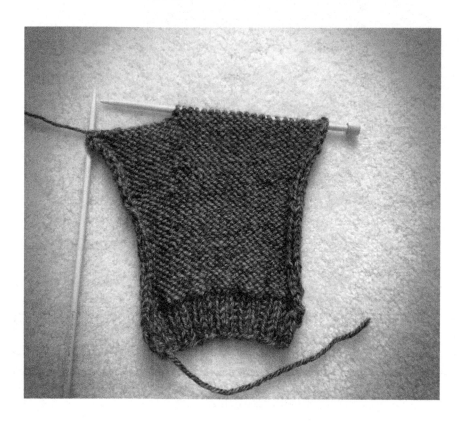

i. Insert the right needle through the front (from left to right) of the end stitch on the left needle.

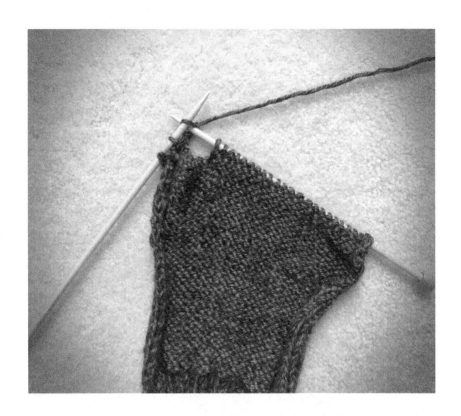

ii. Wind the yarn over the right needle.

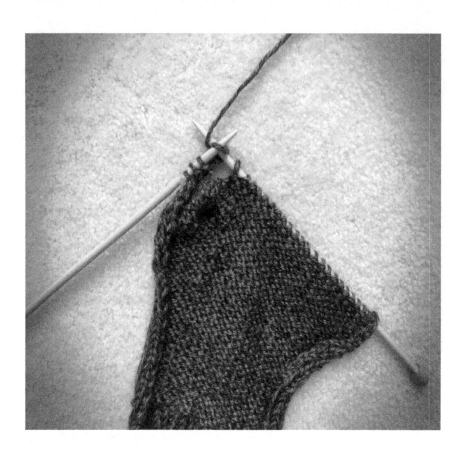

iii. Using the right needle,
pull through the loop.

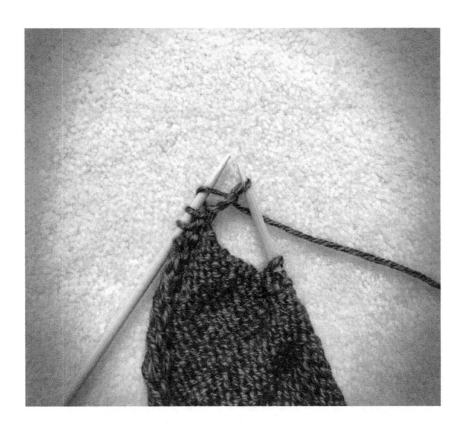

iv. Using the right needle,
place the loop onto the
left needle.

v. Remove right needle from loop and voila! You've just cast on one stitch in the middle of a row.

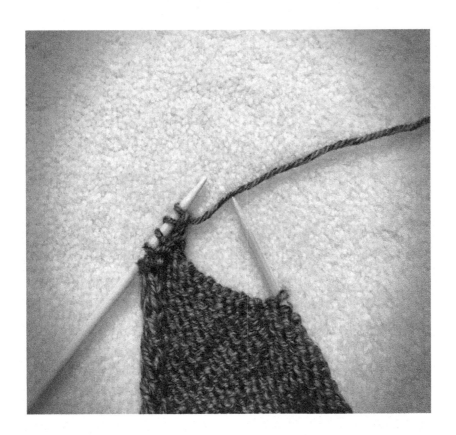

vi. In order to cast on the second stitch in the middle of a row, repeat the above steps. Below are photos in sequence showing the second stitch being cast on.

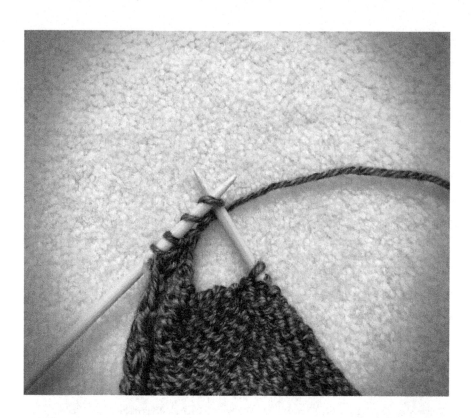

Then turn the work back over again so the knit side is facing up.

Continue to knit to the end of the row, closing the hole you've just created for the thumb.

You should have 26 stitches at the end of this row.

j. <u>Rows 16-24</u>: Knit in stockinette stitch for about 1 ½ inches (9 rows)

k. <u>Rows 25-30</u>: To create the top ribbing, work K2, P2 (rib stitch) for about 1 inch (6 rows).

Step 5: Bind off stitches in rib stitch.

Tip: Use larger needle to bind off in order to keep stitches large and the last row not too tight.

Step 6: Fold the finished piece in half lengthwise, wrong side to wrong side. Use darning needle to sew side seam (use one of the end "tails" or, if "tails" not long enough, cut a long piece of yarn to use to sew seam. Weave in any loose/long ends.

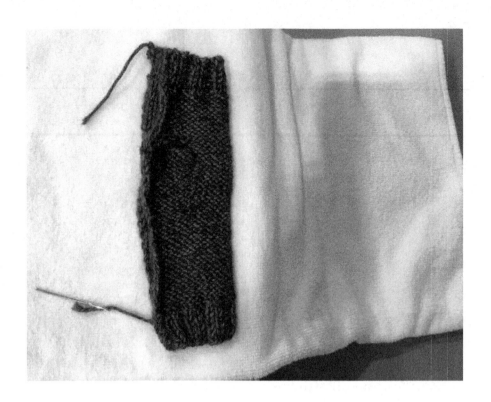

For the upper body hand covering/thumb gusset section on the right mitten:

Step 1: Cast on 28 stitches.

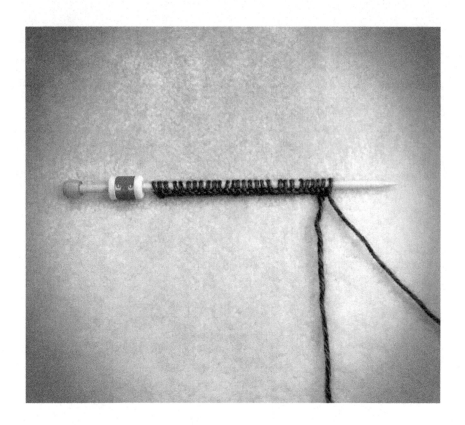

Step 2: To create the bottom ribbing, work K2, P2 (rib stitch), for about 1 inch (6 rows).

Step 3: Then, to create the mitten's lower half (i.e., the section that covers the wrist), work in stockinette stitch for about 3 inches (another 18 rows).

Step 4: Now you're ready to create the upper body hand covering/thumb gusset.

      a. <u>Row 1</u> (This is on the mitten's right- or out-facing side): K21, PM, M1, K6, M1, PM, K1. Since the beginning, you have increased or added two new stitches, bringing the total number of stitches in this row to 30.

b. <u>Rows 2-4</u>: Continue in stockinette stitch.

c. <u>Row 5</u>: K1 to marker, SM, M1, knit to next marker, M1, SM, knit to end of row. You've increased or added two new stitches to this row, bringing the total number of stitches in this row to 32.

d. <u>Rows 6-8</u>: Continue in stockinette stitch.

e. <u>Row 9</u>: Repeat row 5. You've added two new stitches/increase this row to 34 stitches total.

f. <u>Rows 10-12</u>: Continue in stockinette stitch.

g. <u>Row 13</u>: Repeat row 5. You've added two new stitches/increase this row to 36 stitches total, including 14 stitches between markers.

h. <u>Row 14</u>: (WS) Purl to marker, remove marker, P2, bind off 10 stitches for thumb opening, P2, remove marker, and purl to end of row. You should have 26 stitches at the end of this row.

i. <u>Row 15</u>: (RS) Knit, casting on 2 stitches over bound off stitches of previous row. You should have 26 stitches at the end of this row.

j. <u>Rows 16-24</u>: Knit in stockinette stitch for about one and a half inches (9 rows)

k. <u>Rows 25-30</u>: To create the top ribbing, work K2, P2 (rib stitch) for about 1 inch (6 rows).

Step 5: Bind off stitches in rib stitch.

Tip: Use larger needle to bind off in order to keep stitches large and the last row not too tight.

Step 6: Fold the finished piece in half lengthwise, wrong side to wrong side. Use darning needle to sew side seam (use one of the end "tails" or, if "tails" not long enough, cut a long piece of yarn to use to sew seam. Weave in any loose/long ends.

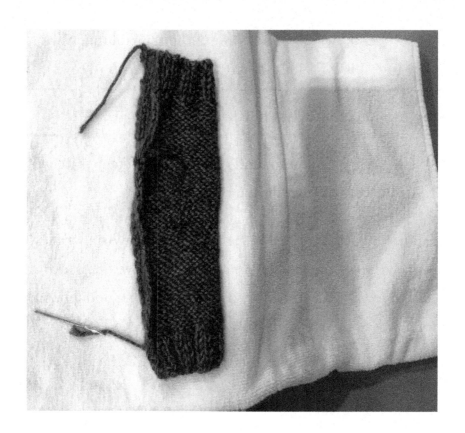

Each mitten's finished circumference at the upper and lower edges is about seven inches.

The finished length from top edge to bottom edge is about nine and a half inches.

Customize the mittens as you wish–lengthen the wrist section for more coverage, shorten the wrist section to less coverage, or add or subtract stitches (but still follow the basic pattern shape) to make it more wide or narrow.

Chose any colors (or even color-patterned yarn) you want to create different looks. As you can see, fingerless mittens are quick, easy, and fun little accessories that make cute and thoughtful gifts.

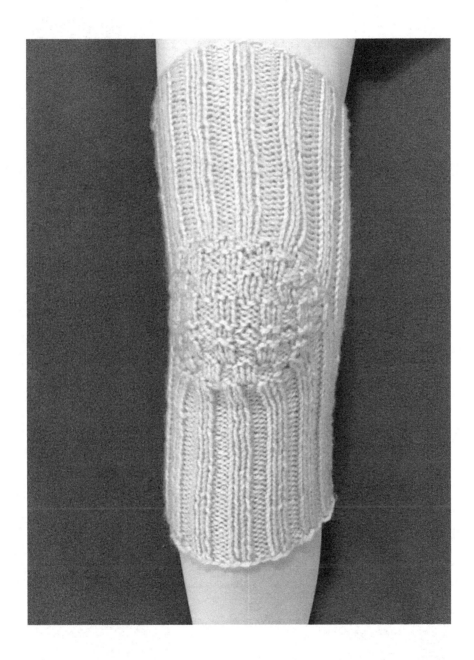

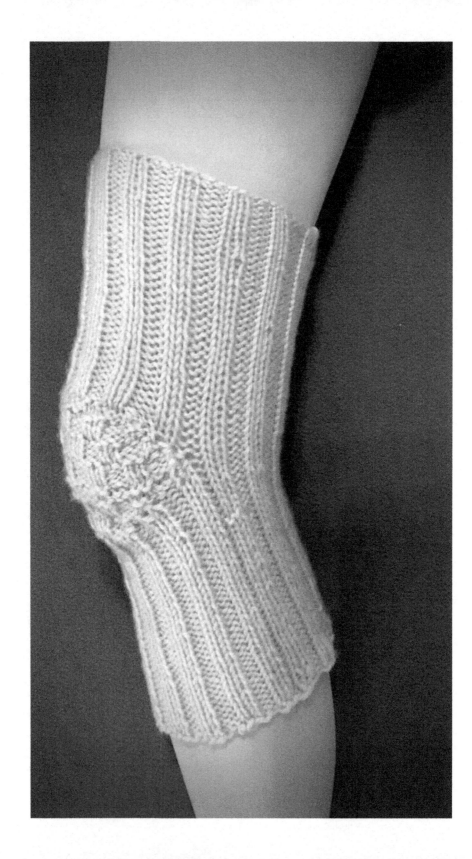

Legwarmers emerged as a popular fad the 1980's–fashionable yet functional. Today, people still wear them because leg warmers are practical, cozy, and comfortable. But what if you only want to keep part of your leg warm? Leg warmers are long, but if only one part (e.g., the knee, calve, or ankle) needs special attention, you don't need an entire leg warmer. Bunching up excess leg-warmer length can create extra bulk.

One day in ballet class, I noticed that a classmate wore a pair of short leg warmers that extended from just above to just below the knees. She wanted to keep her knees warm, so she found children's leg warmers the right length to fit just over her knee area. How clever!

I love this novel idea of repurposing of children's leg warmers for adult knees. Knee warmers are great for people who want to focus on cold knees but don't need warmers for the rest of the leg (e.g., calves or thighs). Also, knee warmers made with lightweight yarn are great for fitting under everyday clothing like pants and long skirts without adding extra bulk.

Of course children's leg warmers might be too narrow for adults, so try the knee warmer pattern for adults below.

The pattern also incorporates a checker-texture patch (made from **short rows**–explained later) in the middle in order to cover the kneecap while still allowing the knee to bend easily. The only minor drawback for some people is that the patch in front of the knee wrinkles when standing straight.

Before you begin working on the Knee Warmers, gather the following materials:

- One skein (at most 5 ounces, 251 yards) of medium worsted weight (4) yarn–acrylic, acrylic-wool blend, or wool. Personally, I like acrylic because it is soft and warm.
- One pair of circular size 5, 16-inch circular knitting needles
- One knitting needle (straight or circular) larger than size 5 for binding off (pictured are size 13 circular needles, but use what you already have)
- Two stitch markers (pictured are more so you can see different sizes; (optional) you can hang "earring-like" decorations from the circular stitch markers like those pictured)
- One large-eye blunt darning needle

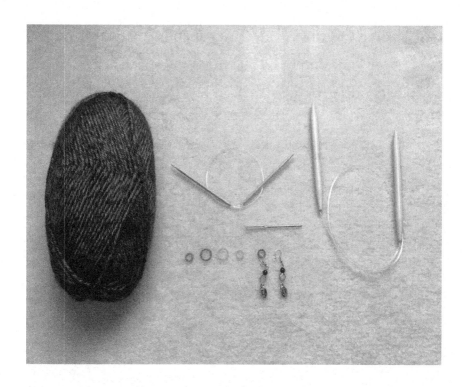

This warmer fits a knee measuring about 14" around. For sizes fitting a 15" knee and an 18" knee, use the numbers in parentheses *(15"#, 18"#)*. This pattern's gauge is 24 stitches equaling about four inches in stockinette stitch. For extra snugness, knit at a firmer gauge.

For this Knee Warmer pattern, you need to know one term in addition to the basic Knit and Purl stitches. The term is **W&T (wrap and turn)**, a technique used to knit short rows within a larger piece. You'll encounter the W&T starting in Row 35. When you're instructed to **W&T**:

1. Leave the yarn draped to whichever side it is on after you completed the previous stitch (e.g., in back after a knit stitch; in front after a purl stitch).

2. Slip the next stitch on the left needle purlwise to the right needle.

3. Move the yarn between the needles to the other side of the project.

4. Slip the slipped stitch back to the left needle.

5. Move the yarn between the needles to the side where it was before.

6. Turn the project around.

To see how to execute W&T, look on YouTube for helpful demonstrations.

Step 1: Cast on 56 *(64,80)* stitches.

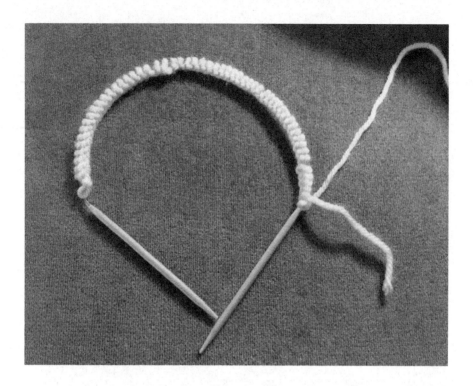

Step 2: Place a stitch marker on the needle with the working yarn tail in order to mark the beginning of a row (or "round" when the row goes all the way around with circular needles).

Step 3:

Row/Round 1: Start working K2, P2 all the way around, joining the ends of the opening and taking care not to twist the row of cast-on stitches.

Step 4:

<u>Rows/Rounds 2-34:</u> K2, P2

Now you've completed the top ribbing.

Step 5: To create the checker-texture patch area that covers the knee cap, you'll work in short rows for the next 31 rows.

- Row 35: Work 44 *(46,50)* stitches in K2P2 ribbing, W&T

- Row 36: (K2, P2) 3 *(4,5)* times, W&T
- Row 37: (K2, P2) 3 *(4,5)* times, K1, W&T

- <u>Row 38</u>: P1, (K2, P2) 3 *(4,5)* times, K1, W&T
- <u>Row 39</u>: P1, (K2, P2) 3 *(4,5)* times, K2, W&T

- <u>Row 40</u>: (K2, P2) 4 *(5,6)* times, W&T

- <u>Row 41</u>: (K2, P2) 4 *(5,6)* times, K1, W&T

- <u>Row 42</u>: P1, (K2, P2) 4 *(5,6)* times, K1, W&T

- <u>Row 43</u>: P1, (K2, P2) 4 *(5,6)* times, K2, W&T

- <u>Row 44</u>: (K2, P2) 5 *(6,7)* times, W&T

- <u>Row 45</u>: (K2, P2) 5 *(6,7)* times, K1, W&T

- <u>Row 46</u>: P1, (K2, P2) 5 *(6,7)* times, K1, W&T

- <u>Row 47</u>: P1, (K2, P2) 5 *(6,7)* times, K2, W&T

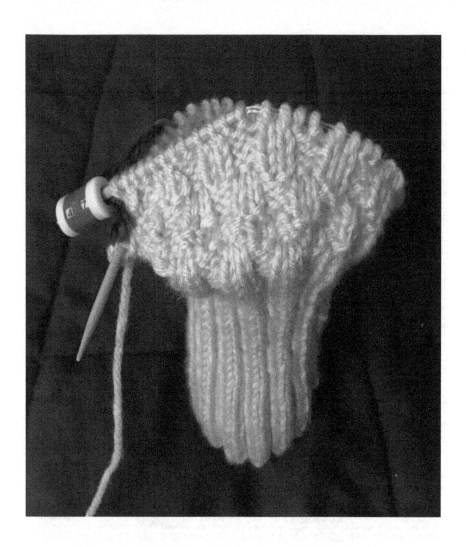

- <u>Row 48</u>: (K2, P2) 6 *(7,8)* times, W&T

- <u>Row 49</u>: (K2, P2) 6 *(7,8)* times, K1, W&T

- <u>Row 50</u>: P1, (K2, P2) 6 *(7,8)* times, K1, W&T

- <u>Row 51</u>: P1, (K2, P2) 6 *(7,8)* times, W&T

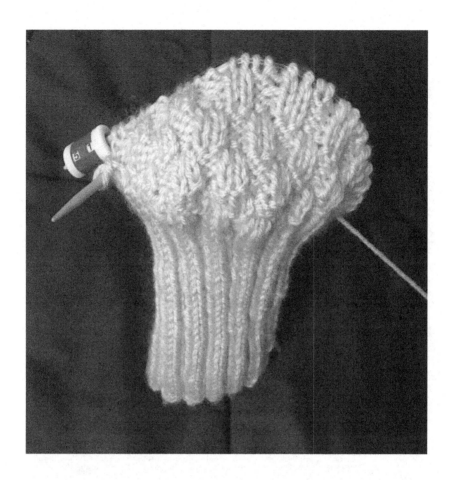

- <u>Row 52</u>: P2, (K2, P2) 5 *(6, 7)* times, K2, W&T

- <u>Row 53</u>: P2, (K2, P2) 5 *(6, 7)* times, K1, W&T

- <u>Row 54</u>: P1, (K2, P2) 5 *(6, 7)* times, K1, W&T

- <u>Row 55</u>: P1, (K2, P2) 5 *(6, 7)* times, W&T

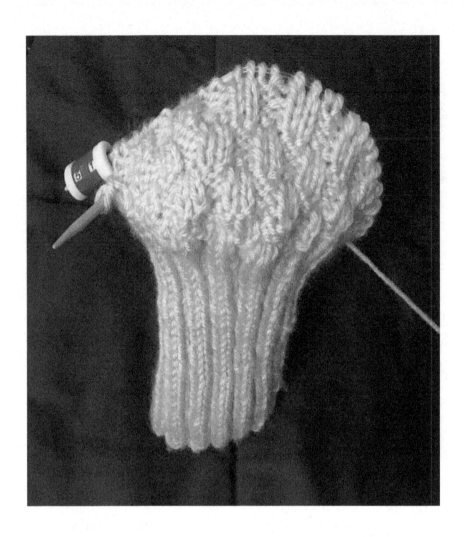

- <u>Row 56</u>: P2, (K2, P2) 4 *(5,6)* times, K2, W&T

- <u>Row 57</u>: P2, (K2, P2) 4 *(5,6)* times, K1, W&T

- <u>Row 58</u>: P1, (K2, P2) 4 *(5,6)* times, K1, W&T

- <u>Row 59</u>: P1, (K2, P2) 4 *(5,6)* times, W&T

- <u>Row 60</u>: P2, (K2, P2) 3 *(4,5)* times, K2, W&T
- <u>Row 61</u>: P2, (K2, P2) 3 *(4,5)* times, K1, W&T
- <u>Row 62</u>: P1, (K2, P2) 3 *(4,5)* times, K1, W&T
- <u>Row 63</u>: P1, (K2, P2) 3 *(4,5)* times, W&T

- <u>Row 64</u>: P2, (K2, P2) 2 *(3,4)* times, K2, W&T
- <u>Row 65</u>: P2, (K2, P2) to end of row/round

Step 6: To create the bottom ribbing, continue Rows/Rounds 66-100 in K2, P2.

** Note: if you ever find that the K2, P2 ribbing rows are off/not matched up with the earlier ribbing, feel free to adjust the K2, P2 counts when needed. In other words–

and only if you find you need to–maybe K1 once instead of K2 or P1 once instead of P2 in order to get the ribbing back on track. If you don't find you need to do this, congrats! **

Step 7: For <u>Row/Round 100</u>, bind off very loosely with larger needle, bind off.

To create a second Knee Warmer for the second leg, just repeat all of the above directions.

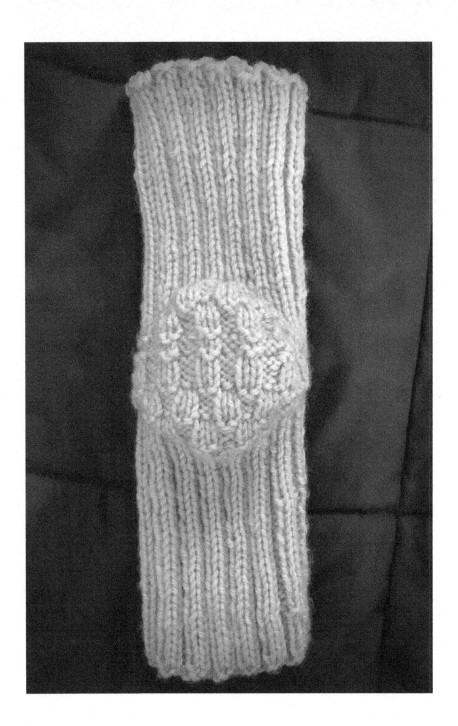

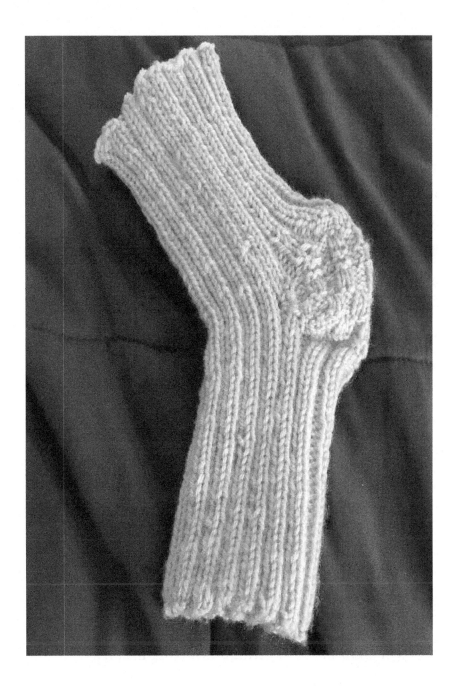

CHAPTER THREE: TRIO OF TEXTURED KITCHEN CLOTHS

The term "kitchen cloth" conjures up images of dingy old rags. The patterns below make this workhorse of the kitchen fashionable yet functional. Practice these subtle variations on simple patterns to create whimsical designs for multipurpose cloths you can use to wipe up spills, wipe down countertops, place under dishes to protect tabletops, and more. These knitting projects are especially rewarding to work on because they're quick, easy, beautiful and useful in the end.

For these three different patterns, you need very little equipment:

- One skein (at most 2.5 ounces, 120 yards) of medium worsted weight (4) 100% cotton yarn. This amount covers at two projects, but you may want to mix it up and choose different colors. Pick any hue you like–bright, earth tone, solid, mixed, etc.
- One pair of size 7 straight knitting needles
- A row counter

These Kitchen Cloth patterns don't need a gauge, because they aren't fitted garments or have to be a specific size. In fact, if you want to make these cloths smaller or larger than the indicated finished sizes, simply go up or down one knitting needle size if needed.

PATTERN ONE: QUARTERS KITCHEN CLOTH

For this Quarters Kitchen Cloth pattern, you need to know one term in addition to the basic Knit and Purl stitches. The term is **Slip**, which means you simply slip (not knit or purl) the stitch onto the other needle.

Cast on 36 stitches.

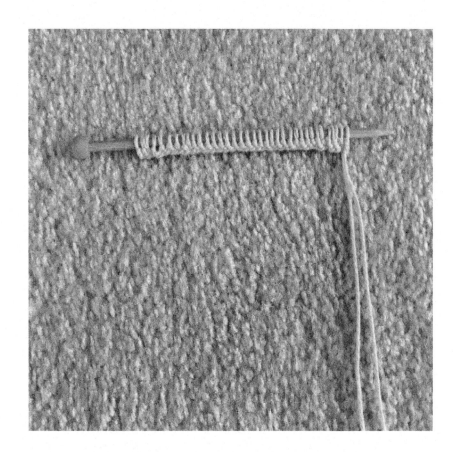

<u>Row 1</u>: Slip 1 stitch, K35

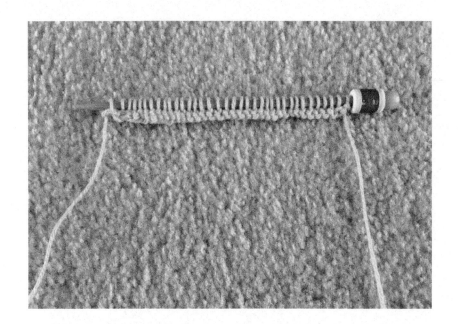

Row 2: Slip 1 stitch, P35

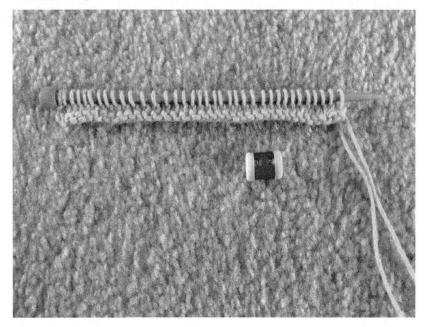

Row 3: Slip 1 stitch, P32, K3

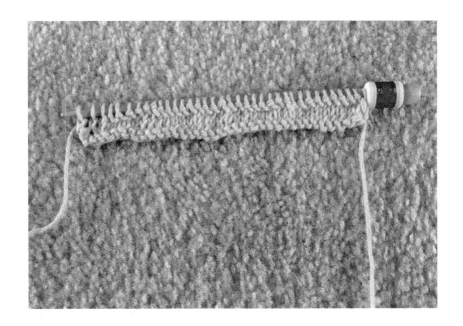

<u>Row 4</u>: Slip 1 stitch, P2, K15, P15, K3

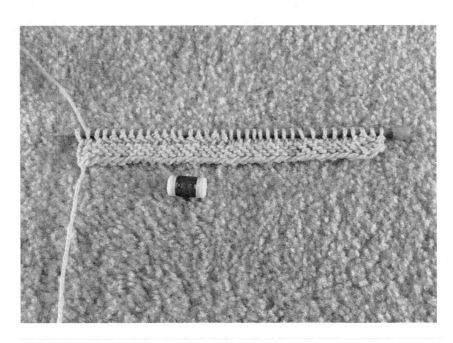

<u>Row 5-22</u>: Slip 1 stitch, P2, K15, P15, K3

<u>Row 23</u>: Slip 1 stitch, K2, P15, K15, P3

Row 24-41: Slip 1 stitch, K2, P15, K15, P3

Row 42: Knit all stitches

Row 43: Purl all stitches

Bind off with loose knit stitches. Weave in or trim tails.

The finished Quarters Kitchen Cloth measures 8.5" x 6.75".

PATTERN TWO: DIAGONALS KITCHEN CLOTH

Enjoy this funky design!

Cast on 38 stitches.

<u>Row 1</u>: P2, K2 to end.

<u>Row 2</u>: K1, then (K2, P2) to last stitch, K1.

Row 3: Use previous row as a guide: knit the knit, purl the purl

Row 4: K1, P1, then (K2, P2) to last 2 stitches, P1, K1

Row 5: Use previous row as a guide: Knit the knit, purl the purl

Row 6: K1, (then P2, K2) to last 3 stitches, K3

Row 7: Use previous row as a guide: Knit the knit, purl the purl

Row 8: K2, P2, then (K2, P2) to last 2 stitches, K2

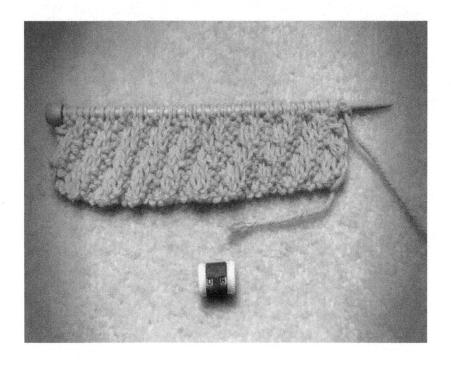

Row 9: Use previous row as a guide: Knit the knit, purl the purl

Row 10: K1, then (K2, P2) to last stitch, K1.

Row 11: Use previous row as a guide: Knit the knit, purl the purl

Row 12: K1, P1, then (K2, P2) to last 2 stitches, P1, K1

Row 13: Use previous row as a guide: Knit the knit, purl the purl

Row 14: K1, (then P2, K2) to last 3 stitches, K3

Row 15: Use previous row as a guide: Knit the knit, purl the purl

Row 16: K2, P2, then (K2, P2) to last 2 stitches, K2

Row 17: Use previous row as a guide: Knit the knit, purl the purl

Row 18: K1, then (K2, P2) to last stitch, K1.

Row 19: Use previous row as a guide: Knit the knit, purl the purl

Row 20: K1, P1, then (K2, P2) to last 2 stitches, P1, K1

Row 21: Use previous row as a guide: Knit the knit, purl the purl

Row 22: K1, (then P2, K2) to last 3 stitches, K3

Row 23: Use previous row as a guide: Knit the knit, purl the purl

Row 24: K2, P2, then (K2, P2) to last 2 stitches, K2

Row 25: Use previous row as a guide: Knit the knit, purl the purl

Row 26: K1, then (K2, P2) to last stitch, K1.

Row 27: Use previous row as a guide: Knit the knit, purl the purl

Row 28: K1, P1, then (K2, P2) to last 2 stitches, P1, K1

Row 29: Use previous row as a guide: Knit the knit, purl the purl

Row 30: K1, (then P2, K2) to last 3 stitches, K3

Row 31: Use previous row as a guide: Knit the knit, purl the purl

Row 32: K2, P2, then (K2, P2) to last 2 stitches, K2

Row 33: Use previous row as a guide: Knit the knit, purl the purl

Row 34: K1, then (K2, P2) to last stitch, K1.

Row 35: Use previous row as a guide: Knit the knit, purl the purl

Row 36: K1, P1, then (K2, P2) to last 2 stitches, P1, K1

Row 37: Use previous row as a guide: Knit the knit, purl the purl

Row 38: K1, (then P2, K2) to last 3 stitches, K3

Row 39: Use previous row as a guide: Knit the knit, purl the purl

Row 40: K2, P2, then (K2, P2) to last 2 stitches, K2

Row 41: Use previous row as a guide: Knit the knit, purl the purl

<u>Row 42</u>: Bind off with loose knit stitches. Weave in or trim tails.

The finished Diagonals Kitchen Cloth measures 9.25" x 6.75".

PATTERN THREE: TINY CHECKERS KITCHEN CLOTH

This design combines ribbing on the top and bottom edges, a knit-stitch column on the left edge, and tiny checkers throughout. If you gaze at the pattern long enough, it looks like knit-stitch rows weave vertically through the purl-stitch rows.

Cast on 38 stitches.

<u>Row 1</u>: P3, then (K2, P2) to last 3 stitches, P3

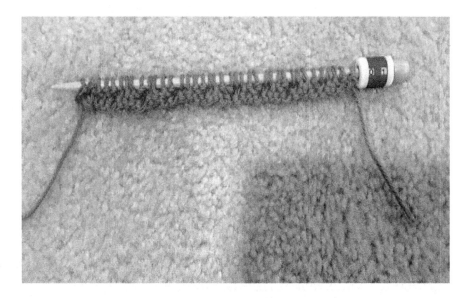

<u>Row 2</u>: K1, then (P2, K2) to last 3 stitches, P2, K1

<u>Row 3</u>: Use previous row as a guide: Knit the knit, purl the purl

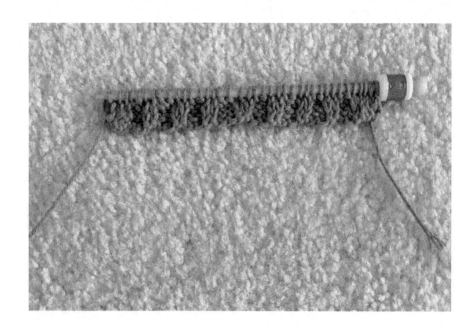

Row 4: K1, then repeat (K2, P2) to last stitch, K1

Row 5: Use previous row as a guide: Knit the knit, purl the purl

Row 6: K1, then (P2, K2) to last 3 stitches, P2, K1

Row 7: Use previous row as a guide: Knit the knit, purl the purl

Row 8: K1, then repeat (K2, P2) to last stitch, K1

Row 9: Use previous row as a guide: Knit the knit, purl the purl

Row 10: K1, then (P2, K2) to last 3 stitches, P2, K1

Row 11: Use previous row as a guide: Knit the knit, purl the purl

Row 12: K1, then repeat (K2, P2) to last stitch, K1

Row 13: Use previous row as a guide: Knit the knit, purl the purl

Row 14: K1, then (P2, K2) to last 3 stitches, P2, K1

Row 15: Use previous row as a guide: Knit the knit, purl the purl

Row 16: K1, then repeat (K2, P2) to last stitch, K1

Row 17: Use previous row as a guide: Knit the knit, purl the purl

Row 18: K1, then (P2, K2) to last 3 stitches, P2, K1

Row 19: Use previous row as a guide: Knit the knit, purl the purl

Row 20: K1, then repeat (K2, P2) to last stitch, K1

Row 21: Use previous row as a guide: Knit the knit, purl the purl

Row 22: K1, then (P2, K2) to last 3 stitches, P2, K1

Row 23: Use previous row as a guide: Knit the knit, purl the purl

Row 24: K1, then repeat (K2, P2) to last stitch, K1

Row 25: Use previous row as a guide: Knit the knit, purl the purl

Row 26: K1, then (P2, K2) to last 3 stitches, P2, K1

Row 27: Use previous row as a guide: Knit the knit, purl the purl

Row 28: K1, then repeat (K2, P2) to last stitch, K1

Row 29: Use previous row as a guide: Knit the knit, purl the purl

Row 30: K1, then (P2, K2) to last 3 stitches, P2, K1

Row 31: Use previous row as a guide: Knit the knit, purl the purl

Row 32: K1, then repeat (K2, P2) to last stitch, K1

Row 33: Use previous row as a guide: Knit the knit, purl the purl

Row 34: K1, then (P2, K2) to last 3 stitches, P2, K1

Row 35: Use previous row as a guide: Knit the knit, purl the purl

Row 36: K1, then repeat (K2, P2) to last stitch, K1

Row 37: Use previous row as a guide: Knit the knit, purl the purl

Row 38: K1, then (P2, K2) to last 3 stitches, P2, K1

<u>Row 39</u>: Use previous row as a guide: Knit the knit, purl the purl

<u>Row 40</u>: Use previous row as a guide: Knit the knit, purl the purl

<u>Row 41</u>: Bind off with loose knit stitches. Weave in or trim tails.

The finished Tiny Checkers Kitchen Cloth measures 9.25" x 6.5".

CHAPTER FOUR: CRISSCROSS COASTERS

The Crisscross Coaster pattern results in a piece slightly thicker and stiffer than the Quarters Kitchen Cloth, the Diagonals Kitchen Cloth, and the Tiny Checkers Kitchen Cloth. The Crisscross Coaster's texture is created by repeatedly a crossing one completed Knit stitch over another Knit stitch.

SUPPLIES YOU WILL NEED

For the Crisscross Coaster, you need very little equipment and supplies:

- One skein (at most 2.5 ounces, 120 yards) of medium worsted weight (4) 100% cotton yarn. This amount accommodates at least six coasters of the same color. Cotton is tough, absorbent, and available in pretty colors, bright hues, earth tones, and many other shades.
- One pair of size 7 straight knitting needles
- A row counter
- One large-eye blunt darning needle

In this pattern, you'll see the direction "Knit second stitch on needle and lift it over the first stitch". No worries–you've become so adept at knitting that this new maneuver is no sweat!

ACTUAL STEP BY STEP PROCESS

How to Knit the Second Stitch on a Needle and Lift it Over the First Stitch

Step 1: With the yarn positioned behind the right needle, insert the right needle through the front (from left to right) of the next-to-last (or second) stitch on the left needle.

Step 2: Wind the yarn over the right needle.

Step 3: Pull through the loop–just as you would when executing any Knit stitch.

<u>Step 4</u>: Lift the Knit stitch you just made OVER the end (or first) stitch on the left needle ...

Step 5: Pull the Knit stitch off of the left needle. Notice how that stitch now crosses over the end stitch?

Step 6: Now knit the end (or first) stitch as you would for any Knit stitch.

Voila! You've taken a step in building a coaster in a Crisscross pattern. The resulting textures are different on each side of the finished project.

One side shows stitches obviously crossing over other stitches.

The other side has more of a nubby appearance.

This Crisscross pattern is versatile because you have two choices of textures to position facing upward when using the finished coaster.

Cast on 22 stitches.

<u>Row 1</u>: P2, K2 until last two stitches; P2

Row 2: K1, then (P2, Knit second stitch on needle and lift it over the first stitch) to last stitch, K1

Two sides of the project through this point:

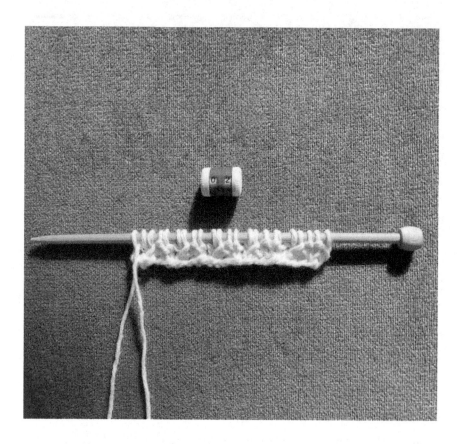

<u>Row 3</u>: P1, K1, then (P2, K2) to last two stitches, K1, P1

<u>Row 4</u>: K1, then (P2, Knit second stitch on needle and lift it over the first stitch) to last stitch, K1

Two sides of the project through this point:

<u>Row 5</u>: P2, K2 until last two stitches, P2

<u>Row 6</u>: K1, then (P2, Knit second stitch on needle and lift it over the first stitch) to last stitch, K1

Two sides of the project through this point:

Row 7: P1, K1, then (P2, K2) to last two stitches, K1, P1

Row 8: K1, then (P2, Knit second stitch on needle and lift it over the first stitch) to last stitch, K1

Row 9: P2, K2 until last two stitches, P2

Row 10: K1, then (P2, Knit second stitch on needle and lift it over the first stitch) to last stitch, K1

Row 11: P1, K1, then (P2, K2) to last two stitches, K1, P1

Row 12: K1, then (P2, Knit second stitch on needle and lift it over the first stitch) to last stitch, K1

Row 13: P2, K2 until last two stitches, P2

<u>Row 14</u>: K1, then (P2, Knit second stitch on needle and lift it over the first stitch) to last stitch, K1

<u>Row 15</u>: P1, K1, then (P2, K2) to last two stitches, K1, P1

<u>Row 16</u>: K1, then (P2, Knit second stitch on needle and lift it over the first stitch) to last stitch, K1

<u>Row 17</u>: P2, K2 until last two stitches, P2

<u>Row 18</u>: K1, then (P2, Knit second stitch on needle and lift it over the first stitch) to last stitch, K1

<u>Row 19</u>: P1, K1, then (P2, K2) to last two stitches, K1, P1

<u>Row 20</u>: K1, then (P2, Knit second stitch on needle and lift it over the first stitch) to last stitch, K1

<u>Row 21</u>: P2, K2 until last two stitches, P2

<u>Row 22</u>: K1, then (P2, Knit second stitch on needle and lift it over the first stitch) to last stitch, K1

<u>Row 23</u>: P1, K1, then (P2, K2) to last two stitches, K1, P1

<u>Row 24</u>: K1, then (P2, Knit second stitch on needle and lift it over the first stitch) to last stitch, K1

<u>Row 25</u>: P2, K2 until last two stitches, P2

<u>Row 26</u>: Bind off with loose knit stitches. Trim tails or weave un tails with darning needle.

One finished Crisscross Coaster measures 4.5" x 4.25".

Since knitting a single coaster doesn't require much yarn, you can make several Crisscross Coasters to create a lovely set. Or mix and match yarn colors to fit your mood or décor. Another idea is to make different sets of a single color for various occasions and seasons.

Finally, you can expand to make a thick kitchen cloth–
simply cast on 38 (instead of 22) stitches and knit more
rows in multiples of four.

CONCLUSION

All of these projects–the Fingerless Mittens, the Knee Warmers, the Trio of Textured Kitchen Cloths, and the Crisscross Coaster–are relatively quick and easy ... but still challenging and interesting enough to test your burgeoning knitting skills.

The projects don't require expensive yarn, like 100% wool or cashmere. Nonetheless, you have plenty of freedom to choose different types and colors of yarn to customize them as you wish.

Knitting is a fabulous activity because it is portable, satisfying, and calming. Take these projects along with you to work on while traveling, waiting for appointments, watching sports games, socializing with friends, and more. Pack a small bag with your knitting supplies (yarn, needles, counter, markers, darning needle, and scissors) so you're ready to knit wherever you are.

And always remember: YouTube is rich with helpful demonstrations of knitting techniques when you need to SEE actual steps of needlework.

Enjoy continuing to advance in this wonderfully productive and useful hobby.

Lastly, if you liked my work, I would love to see a review from you.

Thank you!

Made in the USA
Las Vegas, NV
12 December 2021

37269900R00075